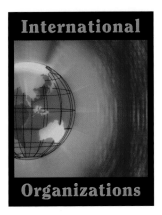

Red Cross and Red Crescent

Jean F. Blashfield

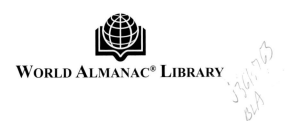

WORLD ALMANAC® LIBRARY

Please visit our web site at: www.worldalmanaclibrary.com
For a free color catalog describing World Almanac® Library's list
of high-quality books and multimedia programs, call 1-800-848-2928 (USA)
or 1-800-387-3178 (Canada). World Almanac® Library's fax: (414) 332-3567.

Library of Congress Cataloging-in-Publication Data

Blashfield, Jean F.
    Red Cross and Red Crescent / by Jean F. Blashfield.
       p. cm. — (International organizations)
    Summary: Describes the history, principles, structure, and activities of the organization
that brings humanitarian relief to the people of the world in both war and peace.
    Includes bibliographical references and index.
    ISBN 0-8368-5521-3 (lib. bdg.)
    ISBN 0-8368-5530-2 (softcover)
    1. Red Cross—Juvenile literature. [1. Red Cross.] I. Title. II. International organizations
(Milwaukee, Wis.)
HV568.B58   2003
361.7'634—dc21   2003047945

First published in 2004 by
World Almanac® Library
330 West Olive Street, Suite 100
Milwaukee, WI 53212 USA

Copyright © 2004 by World Almanac® Library.

Developed by Books Two, Inc.
Editor: Jean B. Black
Design and Maps: Krueger Graphics, Inc.: Karla J. Krueger and Victoria L. Buck
Indexer: Chandelle Black
World Almanac® Library editor: JoAnn Early Macken
World Almanac® Library art direction: Tammy Gruenewald

Photo Credits: American Red Cross: 14, 36, 37, 38; Associated Press: 4; Ayad el Mounzer/Lebanese
Red Cross: 6; © International Committee of the Red Cross: 10, Jessica Barry–23, 31, Boris
Heger–26, 27, Till Mayer–18, John Spraull–30, Marcel Vergeer–28; © The International Federation
of the Red Cross and Red Crescent Societies: Logos–1, 32, 44, Marko Kokic–34, 35, Andrei
Naescu–cover, Mikkel Oestergaard–19, 32, 33, Thorkell Thorkelsson–22; Library of Congress: 13,
15, 16, 40; Magen David Adom: 43; © Photothèque CICR ®/: 11; © Photothèque CICR ®/LE
ROUGE, Georges: 8; Reuters/KEVIN LAMARQUE: 29; Seattle Times Photo from ARC: 39

Printed in the United States of America

1 2 3 4 5 6 7 8 9 07 06 05 04 03

TABLE OF CONTENTS

Chapter One   To Serve the Most Vulnerable   4

Chapter Two *Tutti Fratelli*—We All Are Brothers   8

Chapter Three   Multiple Red Crosses   18

Chapter Four Guardians of Humanitarian Law   23

Chapter Five   The Power of Humanity   32

Chapter Six   Into the Third Century   40

Time Line   45

Glossary   46

To Find Out More   47

Index   48

Words that appear in the glossary are printed in
boldface type the first time they occur in the text.

Chapter One

To Serve the Most Vulnerable

On a warm, summery evening on December 17, 1996, in Lima, Peru, the Japanese ambassador to that South American country gave a large party to celebrate the Japanese emperor's birthday. About five hundred guests came, including many dignitaries—even relatives of Peru's president, Alberto Fujimori, although he himself had not come.

Suddenly, at 8 P.M., fourteen waiters appeared, not with trays but with guns. At the same time, a hole was blasted in a back wall of the building, and other gunmen swarmed in. The gala event had been taken over by the *Movimiento Revolucionario Tupac Amaru* (MRTA), called the Tupac Amaru, which means "royal serpent." They demanded the release of more than four hundred imprisoned MRTA members as well as improvements in prison conditions.

Over the next few days, **hostages** were released until a core group of seventy-two diplomats and government officials remained under the guns. Fujimori, who had claimed that terrorism was dead in Peru, refused to **negotiate**. Then, for 126 days, the only contact the hostages had with the outside world was a delegate

A Red Cross officer carried Christmas dinners to people being held hostage in the Japanese Embassy in Lima, Peru, in 1996.

of the International Committee of the Red Cross. The Committee is known and respected the world over for its neutrality—its ability to carry out life-saving tasks without taking one side or the other.

A representative of the International Committee brought in food, fresh clothing, medical supplies, and eventually messages from the hostages' families. He carried out garbage and more messages. The chief Committee delegate, who was trusted by both sides, worked twenty-hour days for week after exhausting week.

Throughout the long ordeal, gunmen and hostages alike were annoyed by regular military displays and loud marching bands playing outside the house. The bands covered up the sounds of tunnels being dug from neighboring houses to the ambassador's residence. On April 22, 1997, 140 commandos invaded the house and rescued the hostages.

Working Under the Banner

No one was surprised that the Red Cross had played such an important role in seeing that the hostages were cared for. This worldwide organization has been doing such things for 140 years. Somewhere in the world, at any time, people carry out important tasks under a banner bearing the symbol of a red cross or a red crescent.

The names "Red Cross" and "Red Crescent" (used in Muslim and a few other countries) actually refer to many different organizations. The go-between in the Peruvian hostage situation worked for the "granddaddy organization," the International Committee of the Red Cross (ICRC). The ICRC is a Swiss corporation that has dealt in **humanitarian** aid since its founding by Swiss businessman Henry Dunant (sometimes referred to as Jean Henri Dunant), who was horrified at the avoidable death he saw on a battlefield. The ICRC reflects Switzerland's own neutrality and is usually allowed to give aid to all warring parties of a conflict.

Across the world, 190 nations are part of the Red Cross and Red Crescent Movement, and most have their own Red Cross or Red Crescent

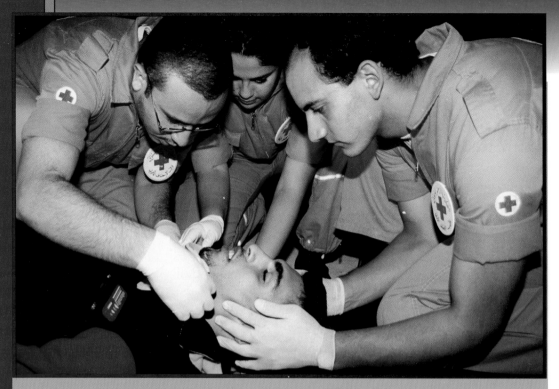

The work of the Red Cross at local events, such as this traffic accident in Lebanon, is carried out by volunteers of the national society.

national society. Each society directs its own activities, especially in disaster relief. In general, the national societies carry out all humanitarian functions, when and where needed (except in war zones) when neutrality is needed to save lives. Each society also works with the International Federation of Red Cross and Red Crescent Societies (IFRC). The IFRC promotes and coordinates the activities of all the national societies in dealing with disasters.

The International Federation and the International Committee, along with all of the national societies, make up the International Red Cross and Red Crescent Movement. All of them function under the same seven Fundamental Principles.

In this book, "Red Cross" means the entire organization and its Movement, unless a specific group—the ICRC, the IFRC, or an individual national society, such as the American Red Cross—is named.

The Fundamental Principles
of the Red Cross and Red Crescent Movement

In 1965, the Conference of the International Red Cross and Red Crescent Movement formulated these seven Fundamental Principles on which all national societies must function.

HUMANITY: The International Red Cross & Red Crescent Movement, born of a desire to bring assistance without discrimination to the wounded on the battlefield, endeavors, in its international and national capacity, to prevent and **alleviate** human suffering wherever it may be found. Its purpose is to protect life and health and to ensure respect for the human being. It promotes mutual understanding, friendship, cooperation and lasting peace amongst all peoples.

IMPARTIALITY: It makes no discrimination as to nationality, race, religious beliefs, class or political opinions. It endeavors to relieve the suffering of individuals, being guided solely by their needs and to give priority to the most urgent cases of distress.

NEUTRALITY: In order to continue to enjoy the confidence of all, the Movement may not take sides in hostilities or engage at any time in controversies of a political, racial, religious or ideological nature.

INDEPENDENCE: The Movement is independent. The National Societies, while auxiliaries in the humanitarian services of their governments and subject to the laws of their respective countries, must always maintain their **autonomy** so that they may be able at all times to act in accordance with the principles of the Movement.

VOLUNTARY SERVICE: It is a voluntary relief movement not prompted in any manner by desire for gain.

UNITY: There can only be one Red Cross or Red Crescent Society in any one country. It must be open to all. It must carry on its humanitarian work throughout its territory.

UNIVERSALITY: The International Red Cross and Red Crescent Movement, in which all Societies have equal status and share equal responsibilities and duties in helping each other, is worldwide.

Chapter Two

Tutti Fratelli—We All Are Brothers

In the middle of the nineteenth century, Europe was in turmoil. Countries were forming and dissolving. People were on the move, and war after war broke out. The effect of one battle is still felt today. The Battle of Solferino was one of several that took place in northern Italy in 1859. Austria-Hungary controlled a large part of northeast Italy. A revolutionary named Garibaldi, with the help of the French, was trying to break that control and liberate the region called Lombardy. Solferino was a small village, but the battle that took place near it on June 24, 1859, was not small. Three hundred thousand Austrian and French soldiers faced each other. By day's end, the Austrians were in retreat. Thousands of dead lay in the village and on the nearby plains. Thousands more wounded lay among them, dying from thirst and untreated wounds.

A young Swiss businessman named Henry Dunant arrived in the area

In this painting, villagers help the wounded at the Battle of Solferino in 1859.

and gave in to his curiosity about what a battle was like. Exploring Solferino, he was appalled by the sights, sounds, and smells. Dunant later wrote, "Bodies of men and horses covered the battlefield; corpses were strewn over roads, ditches, ravines, thickets and fields; the approaches to Solferino were literally thick with dead. The poor wounded men . . . begged to be put out of their misery; and writhed with faces distorted in the grip of the death struggle. . . ."

He was alarmed that no one was paying attention to the wounded, who were rapidly dying. He organized some local women into groups that carried food and water to those who were still alive and washed those whose wounds needed treating. He heard the women whisper, as if reminding themselves, *"Tutti fratelli"* —"we all are brothers."

On his return to his hometown of Geneva, Switzerland, Dunant wrote a small book, *A Memory of Solferino,* as if in a fever. When it was done, he used his own money to have 1,600 copies printed. He gave them to friends, who sent them to influential people all over Europe. In the midst of descriptions of what he had seen, Dunant asked an important question: "Would it not be possible, in time of peace and quiet, to form relief societies for the purpose of having care given to the wounded in wartime by zealous, devoted, and thoroughly qualified volunteers?"

The reaction was stunning. Dunant and his ideas became widely known and appreciated. Apparently the world—all the way up to the royal families of Europe—was ready to react against war. The impact of Dunant's book has been compared to that of Harriet Beecher Stowe's *Uncle Tom's Cabin* on the issue of slavery.

One Geneva man who read a copy of *Memory* was a young lawyer, Gustave Moynier. Moynier invited Dunant to the Geneva Society for Public Welfare. Also in attendance were two doctors, Louis Appia and Théodore Maunoir. Another member, General Guillaume Henri Dufour, a Swiss hero, knew from firsthand experience what it was like to be wounded in battle. This group, along with several others, agreed to form

This old picture shows the founders of the International Red Cross.

the International Committee for Relief to the Wounded.

This group of thoughtful men developed a plan for a permanent corps of volunteer medical personnel and planned a European conference on the subject. Dunant introduced the idea that medical personnel should somehow be accepted as neutral figures. They should not be attached to either party in a war. Moynier thought that such an idea would never be accepted, but he was wrong.

Sixteen nations and four social organizations sent representatives to the conference in Geneva. Not everyone was enthusiastic. One leader thought governments wanting to help should spend their efforts on supplying mules. The idea was adopted, however: doctors and nurses would be neutral, and they and their vehicles would be recognized by showing a red-colored cross on a white background. They did not see it as a Christian symbol; it was just the reverse of the Swiss flag.

The humanitarian decisions made at that meeting came to be called the First Geneva Convention. France was the first nation to sign the 1864 treaty officially called the Geneva Convention for the **Amelioration** of the Condition of the Wounded in Armies in the Field. Within months, eight national societies had been formed, signing a treaty between the International Committee and the government of each nation agreeing to obey the Geneva Convention in the event of war. Among the first non-European national societies were those founded in the Ottoman Empire (later shrunk to Turkey) in 1868, Peru in 1879, and Japan in 1886.

Testing the Idea

The humanitarian ideas were tested in the 1866 war between Austria and Prussia. The Prussians appeared to be following the new rules; the Austrians did not. That same year, in a battle between Austria and Italy, it became clear that battles at sea also had to be included in the Geneva Convention. At the Second Geneva Convention, held in 1868, that idea was added. Also added were the ideas that the wounded themselves should be regarded as neutral

A Red Cross ambulance in Serbia is shown in one of the earliest known photos taken of the Red Cross at work, probably in 1876.

and that soldiers should wear identity tags so the dead and wounded could be identified.

The first complete test of the Geneva Conventions was the Franco-Prussian War in 1870. Both France and Prussia had Red Cross societies. Societies in other countries were ready to provide medical assistance. The Committee in Geneva was also ready—and hopeful.

Red Cross volunteers from many countries became involved. They took over hospitals, turned railroad stations and palaces into more hospitals, and operated in open fields. Prussian soldiers held Paris captive for 131 days, cutting off all supplies to the city. The soldiers did not understand who these people were who were offering help, but the volunteers were able to give assistance to many people. The founders were certain they were on the right track.

The ICRC was formed while the United States was involved in its own civil war. President Abraham Lincoln formed the U.S. Sanitary Commission in 1861, not to care for the wounded but to prevent disease from killing thousands more in the army camps. Most of the work was done by women. This was a first attempt to care for soldiers' health.

"Angel of the Battlefield"

Clara Barton was a Massachusetts woman who was working in Washington, D.C., as a copier at the U.S. Patent Office during the Civil War, one of the few women employed by the government. She was drawn to the nearby battlefields to give what help she could to the wounded, earning her the name "Angel of the Battlefield." Unlike most volunteers, though, she did not stop when the war ended in 1865. She worked for several years to reunite missing soldiers and their families.

Exhausted and ill, Barton was sent to Europe for her health in 1870. She was in Switzerland when her presence was discovered by Dr. Appia. The Red Cross had heard of her, but she had never heard of the Red Cross. Appia asked her to help get the United States to sign the Geneva

Convention. She hadn't heard of the Convention either, but when Dr. Appia explained it, Barton did not understand why the United States would not sign the treaty. She was very impressed when she visited Basle, Switzerland, and saw huge warehouses of materials contributed by Red Cross societies throughout Europe for use in the coming Franco-Prussian War.

Barton was ill for several more years after her return to America, but when her health improved, she actively began to **lobby** the federal government to support the Geneva Convention. President George Washington had once warned citizens of the new United States of America against "entangling alliances," and the government was still avoiding

Clara Barton (1821–1912) founded the American Red Cross.

long-term agreements with other nations. Barton was confident that President James Garfield would sign the Convention, so she went ahead and officially formed the American Association of the Red Cross in May 1881. The first local Red Cross chapter was founded at Dansville, New York, on August 22, 1881. Garfield was assassinated before he could sign, but his successor, Chester Arthur, approved the Convention in March 1882. The Senate **ratified** the treaty two weeks later.

Although the Red Cross organizations were formed for war, Clara Barton thought in terms of providing whatever help was needed, even during peacetime. Within weeks after the American Red Cross (ARC) was formed, Barton called on it to deal with a natural disaster. Summer heat and drought in Michigan caused serious forest fires that left thousands homeless. The ARC provided tents and food. It followed with aid to towns flooded by the rampaging Mississippi River in 1884. Young people became active in the Red Cross when children in Waterford, Pennsylvania, raised money to help families left homeless by those Mississippi River floods.

Barton reported to the Third International Conference of the Red Cross in 1884 that the American Red Cross was working on peacetime disaster relief as well as on the military assistance decreed by the Geneva Convention. The delegates to the conference voted to **amend** the Convention to include such peacetime humanitarian principles. They called it the American Amendment.

The ARC was not called on to help out in an actual war situation until 1898, during the Spanish-American War. Its work in that war led to the American Red Cross being officially **chartered** by the U.S. Congress in 1900. This government charter gave it the recognition it needed to meet all disasters involving American people. The charter was withdrawn, however, when it became known that the Red Cross's internal affairs were in serious disarray. Clara Barton wanted to keep control of everything herself, but she was not good at keeping accounts of dona-

An ambulance driver and a horseback rider wait outside the office of the American Red Cross at Camp Thomas, Georgia, during the Spanish-American War.

San Francisco's 1906 earthquake gave the American Red Cross its first experience in dealing with a huge disaster. This scene is part of an old panoramic photograph of the ruined city.

tions and expenditures. One of the great humanitarians of the world was forced, at age 82, to resign as president of her own organization.

After being reorganized by Barton's successor, Mabel Boardman, the organization was granted a new federal charter in 1905. The American Red Cross was at the front of the aid given to residents of San Francisco after the giant 1906 earthquake, which killed hundreds of people and left more than 250,000 homeless as fires raged across the wooden buildings of the city. The 29-year-old Japanese Red Cross collected almost $150,000 for the American Red Cross's use in San Francisco.

World War and the League

As war loomed in 1914, President Woodrow Wilson asked banker Henry P. Davison to head the American Red Cross War Council. Davison's task was to enlarge the ARC from a $5 million organization to one with an annual expenditure of $50 million. Davidson set a fund-raising goal of an almost unimaginable $100 million.

Join now!

The Red Cross serves humanity

A World War I Red Cross poster recruited nurses for the war effort.

Davison told the American people: "Our job in the American Red Cross is to bind up the wounds of a bleeding world. . . . Think Red Cross! Talk Red Cross! Be Red Cross!" Within less than a year, more than $114 million had been donated. Eventually, the American Red Cross spent more than $330 million during World War I. (In 2000, the American Red Cross had a budget of almost $3 billion.)

At the time Davison became involved in the American Red Cross, there were about 22,000 members nationwide. Within a year, that number had climbed to more than 286,000. By the end of the war, 3,864 chapters had been formed throughout the nation, and twenty million adults and eleven million young people had joined.

As the war started, the ICRC called on the thirty-eight existing societies for help. Within weeks, the American Red Cross's Mercy Ship, filled with supplies, sailed for Europe. Also aboard were 170 surgeons and nurses who would serve throughout Europe. At first, Red Cross workers and supplies were stopped by Germany and other nations who regarded them as being part of the military. The ARC decided to pull all people and supplies out of the combatant countries. Within months, though, it became clear that millions of civilians were suffering. They were starving and stricken by fatal contagious diseases. The American Red Cross moved back into the war zones, where workers could actively help the people they had come to Europe to assist.

Also as the war started, the ICRC established the International Prisoner-of-War Agency. The ICRC had recognized a serious gap in the Geneva Convention—protection for prisoners of war and for civilians who had come under the control of an enemy power. These protections were added to the Geneva Conventions after the war.

The International Committee remained a purely Swiss group with strict adherence to neutrality. The national societies throughout the world had no voice in the decisions of the Committee, so Davison set about forming an international Red Cross organization that would play the major role in rehabilitating the nations and peoples of Europe. He called it the League of Red Cross Societies.

For a period of several years, the Committee and League were, in effect, rivals. This problem sorted itself out when the two organizations defined their missions more clearly. The Committee was to retain what it had originally been organized to do—namely, to work during war. The League was to develop new peacetime activities, such as disaster relief, education, training of nurses, and growth of the Junior Red Cross.

In 1983, the name of the League was expanded to the League of Red Cross and Red Crescent Societies. In November 1991, the organization's name was changed to the International Federation of Red Cross and Red Crescent Societies, or IFRC. (Throughout the remainder of this book, the organization of societies is called the Federation or the IFRC, even when referring to a time when it was officially the League.)

Together, the Committee and the Federation have spent many decades bringing humanitarian relief to the people of the world in war, peace, and natural disaster.

**MAY 8
is World Red Cross and Red Crescent Day because it was Henry Dunant's birthday.**

Chapter Three

Multiple Red Crosses

The several different "Red Cross" organizations work both separately and together. The International Committee of the Red Cross (ICRC) concentrates its efforts on the suffering caused by war. It also promotes acceptance of the Geneva Conventions. The International Federation of Red Cross and Red Crescent Societies (IFRC) responds to nonwar disasters, such as hurricanes, floods, and famines, and also brings aid to **refugees** who have escaped to other countries from war zones. The members of the Federation are the national Red Cross or Red Crescent societies. Almost every nation has a Red Cross or Red Crescent Society.

These three together—Committee, Federation, and national societies—make up the International Red Cross and Red Crescent Movement. Major decisions affecting all of them are made by the international conferences, which meet every four years. Also in attendance at the conferences are representatives of all nations that signed the Geneva Conventions. The ICRC, IFRC, and national societies also meet every two years as the Council of Delegates.

At a conference, governments and societies sit as equals, each with one vote, regardless of their size. The societies agree to abide by the decisions of the conference, but the conference can only give advice. It has no authority to enforce that advice. A permanent Standing Commission of nine members meets to carry out decisions of the

A girl in Guatemala stands by a vehicle bearing the emblem of the International Committee of the Red Cross.

Conference, to discuss any problems that arise between meetings, and to decide when and where the next meeting will take place.

The Use of the Emblems

The red cross or red crescent emblem is used in two ways: first, the emblem indicates that a person or place displaying it can provide assistance and is connected to the Red Cross and Red Crescent Movement. The same emblem is used by the armed forces medical services of the country involved. The second way the emblem is used is as a protection. A person or place displaying it is expected to be given the safety of the Geneva Conventions.

In general, an emblem meant as an indicator is smaller than one meant as a protection. A national society must use one emblem or the other, the red cross or the red crescent. About 15 percent of the nations use the red crescent emblem. Only the Federation uses both. The ICRC, because it is a strictly Swiss organization, uses only the red cross as its emblem. In coming years, the emblems are likely to change, but their meaning will not.

The International Committee

The International Committee employs more than ten thousand people working in seventy-two countries around the world plus about eight hundred in the headquarters in Geneva,

IFRC workers in Turkey after a severe earthquake in 2001 wore the joint red cross and red crescent emblem.

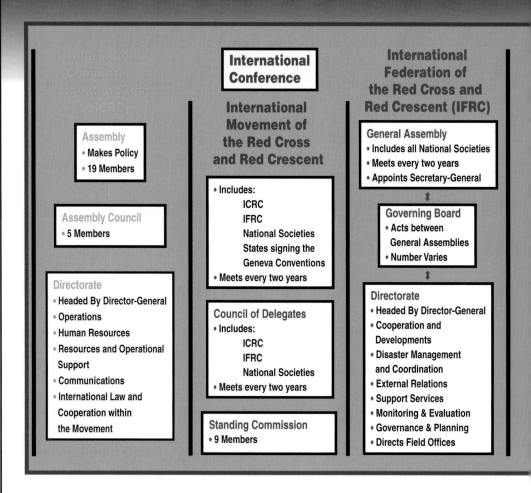

International Committee of the Red Cross (ICRC)

Assembly
- Makes Policy
- 19 Members

Assembly Council
- 5 Members

Directorate
- Headed By Director-General
- Operations
- Human Resources
- Resources and Operational Support
- Communications
- International Law and Cooperation within the Movement

International Conference

International Movement of the Red Cross and Red Crescent

- Includes:
  ICRC
  IFRC
  National Societies
  States signing the Geneva Conventions
- Meets every two years

Council of Delegates
- Includes:
  ICRC
  IFRC
  National Societies
- Meets every two years

Standing Commission
- 9 Members

International Federation of the Red Cross and Red Crescent (IFRC)

General Assembly
- Includes all National Societies
- Meets every two years
- Appoints Secretary-General

Governing Board
- Acts between General Assemblies
- Number Varies

Directorate
- Headed By Director-General
- Cooperation and Developments
- Disaster Management and Coordination
- External Relations
- Support Services
- Monitoring & Evaluation
- Governance & Planning
- Directs Field Offices

Switzerland. Delegations exist in about sixty countries. The people who work for them are referred to as delegates. Their task is to keep an eye out for events that may lead to war and to prepare the ICRC to leap into action if necessary. The United States pays about one-fourth of the ICRC's operations budget.

Even though the Committee is a Swiss corporation, it is completely independent of the Swiss or any other government (including that of the United States) and is completely neutral. It reports only to the Red Cross Conference.

The director-general since the summer of 2002 has been Angelo Gnaedinger, a Swiss lawyer who joined the ICRC in 1984. The director-general and the directors under him or her are appointed by the Assembly for four-year terms.

Regional Field Offices of the Federation

The International Federation

From its headquarters—also in Geneva, Switzerland—the International Federation oversees the activities of its current membership of 178 national Red Cross and Red Crescent societies. Each of these societies was approved by the International Committee of the Red Cross as adhering to the Fundamental Principles before being accepted for membership as an organization authorized to carry out its functions under the Red Cross or Red Crescent banner.

In addition to the societies, the IFRC has more than sixty delegations distributed throughout the world. From these locations, they can respond quickly to help the national societies—or the International Committee—in the event of disasters. The map above shows how they are organized into regions.

Two Equal Organizations

The International Committee of the Red Cross and the International Federation of the Red Cross became two equal organizations under the Conference of the International Red Cross Movement. Much of their work is identical—providing food, housing, and medical care for people in need. This situation sometimes put the two organizations in conflict. At a meeting in Seville, Spain, in 1997, the ICRC and the IFRC came to an agreement that places the Committee as the lead agency for international operations in situations of conflict. If the conflict is strictly within a country, the national society of that country is the lead organization.

Both the ICRC and the Federation are responsible for verifying that national societies are able to conduct their activities in line with the Fundamental Principles. Once a national society has passed this hurdle, it is free to join the Federation. The Federation coordinates the work of the national societies in dealing with natural and technological disasters, health emergencies, and refugees.

It isn't always easy to define when relief work involves war and when it does not. The two organizations negotiate with each other to sort out who does what in any situation that might involve both.

Representatives of both the International Committee and a Red Crescent society worked at a refugee camp in Jordan where a foreign worker who had been living in Iraq sought safety in 2003. The aid workers helped him establish communications with his family in Iraq.

Guardians of Humanitarian Law

Since its founding, the main function of the International Committee of the Red Cross has been the alleviation of suffering during war. On one day in early 2003, ICRC delegates worked in eighty conflicts around the world.

In some of these situations, the ICRC is purely getting ready—"just in case."

For example, in 2002, it began to look as if the United States and its allies were going to invade Iraq in order to eliminate weapons of mass destruction. The Committee began to move supplies into warehouses in Iraq and in surrounding countries. Also, its representatives began to meet with officials in both Iraq and the White House to prepare plans for the event of war. As soon as the first battlefield injuries were inflicted and the first prisoners of war were taken in March 2003, Committee delegates were at work.

The International Committee has tasks of many different kinds to carry out in Gaza, a seemingly permanent war zone. In 2001, they distributed relief parcels to people whose homes had been demolished.

The basis for the ICRC being able to provide relief to both sides during war situations and to question the care of prisoners of war is the neutrality stemming from the Geneva Conventions. These treaties between the ICRC and the nations of the world have been evolving since the first ones were written in 1864. The Geneva Conventions were rewritten after World War II, when it was seen how inhumanely people were treated in both the European and Pacific theaters of war.

Virtually all nations on earth—190 of them—have ratified the Geneva Conventions of 1949. The most recent to ratify them were Cook Islands, Eritrea, and Cyprus.

The Additional Protocols

In addition to the Geneva Conventions are two extra treaties called the Additional Protocols, or diplomatic agreements. The situations they cover basically arose as important after 1949. The first emphasizes the need for any army to distinguish between civilians and combatants. This distinction became necessary because of the increase in **guerrilla warfare** and the development of weapons that carry their killing effect far beyond the battlefield. The First Additional Protocol has been signed by 160 nations. The United States signed it, but the Senate has never taken up the issue of ratification.

The Second Protocol gives the same kind of protections to participants and civilians in civil war (or "non-international armed conflicts") as the Geneva Conventions. It has been signed by 153 nations. The U.S.

Senate has not ratified it, either.

Nations that have nuclear weapons regard the Additional Protocols as covering only conventional weapons. In 1996, however, the International Court of Justice declared that the humanitarian rules are the same for the use of nuclear weapons and conventional weapons.

The Geneva Conventions describe what acts constitute a **breach** of the Conventions. The Additional Protocols make some acts criminal.

The Geneva Conventions
A Summary

The First Geneva Convention protects wounded and sick combatants on land, regardless of which nation they belong to, as well as medical and religious personnel. Captured personnel cannot be murdered, tortured, or used in biological experiments.

The Second Geneva Convention protects combatants at sea in the same way.

The Third Geneva Convention requires prisoners of war to be humanely treated. They are to be given adequate housing, food, clothing, and medical care. War correspondents (reporters) and others authorized to travel with the military are protected in the same way.

The Fourth Geneva Convention protects civilians from being treated as military targets. They are to be allowed to continue to live their normal lives as much as possible.

All together, the four Conventions contain 429 articles that detail the protections and give the Committee the right to carry out humanitarian assistance.

International Humanitarian Law

The ICRC asks the two sides in conflict to respect International Humanitarian Law, or IHL. IHL is a combination of humanitarian principles held by most people and international treaties.

Of course, just because International Humanitarian Law exists and has been backed by almost every government does not mean that it is always followed. In fact, warfare is becoming less formal and being left more in the hands of guerrillas and other nontraditional fighting units. This means that there are more breaches of the law today. One of the most important tasks of ICRC delegates around the world is to call attention to these violations and remind the governments involved that they signed the Conventions and Protocols.

There was no real way to punish people responsible for violations of the Conventions until the opening of the International Criminal Court (ICC) in 2003. Although the United States helped develop the court, it

These soldiers in Colombia are attending a special class about the importance of following International Humanitarian Law.

did not ratify the Rome Treaty that created the ICC. When countries join international governmental organizations, such as the UN, they must give up some of their sovereignty, or ultimate authority. The administration felt that there were not enough safeguards built in to protect the sovereignty of nations.

Does the International Humanitarian Law apply to such terrible acts of terrorism as the hijacking of four passenger planes on September 11, 2001, and the consequent killing of three thousand people? Probably not, says the Red Cross, because the terrorist acts were not carried out by a government against its own people or another government but by a separate network of individuals. This means other types of law must apply to terrorist organizations if they are to be stopped and punished.

Delegates at Work

The people who work for the International Committee are located in many countries around the world to keep tabs on what is happening so that they can warn the Committee in advance if the Committee's work is likely to be needed. Most relief organizations exist only when the need becomes obvious. The ICRC is always ready to go into action. It has developed a permanent organization of medical and other personnel located around the world who are willing to leave at a moment's notice.

One massive strike in a civil war may send thousands of people on the road to try to escape the killing. These refugees need help finding safety, and they need food and

The Question of Neutrality

People ask why the ICRC places so much emphasis on neutrality. Isn't this just a way of not having to take a stand on one side or another and to make a moral judgment about a situation?

The ICRC replies, "Neutrality is not an end in itself, but rather a means toward an end, which is: to be able to act on behalf of people protected by humanitarian law and to make a positive difference to those who are affected by armed violence. Neutrality means making no judgment about the merits of one person's need as against another's; it does not mean condoning violations of IHL."

shelter while they remain in protected areas. If relief workers think too much about the huge numbers of people they have to deal with, they may become fearful that they can't do enough. Instead, they concentrate on what they can do at the moment for one person or one family.

During the war in Bosnia in 1993, a Canadian delegate was responsible for feeding more than a half million people. "This job is incredibly frustrating, challenging, aggravating and rewarding," Kasandra Milne told *Maclean's* magazine. "The joyous moments are seeing the convoys [of relief supplies] arrive, and the end of the day when no one on my staff gets hurt."

Unfortunately, it's not unusual for ICRC delegates to be hurt while carrying out their duties. They have no guarantees

A Red Cross aid worker talked with UN peacekeeping troops in the Bosnian town of Brcko in 2000.

of safety other than that provided by the international acceptance of their red cross or red crescent symbols. They do not carry weapons. They are not protected by military units. Throughout the twentieth century, many relief workers were killed during their operations. One delegate was killed in Baghdad in 2003 when caught in the crossfire of a battle.

In one year, 1996, nine delegates were murdered, three in Burundi and six in Chechnya. But at the same time in Chechnya, delegates delivered ten thousand children's packages, each containing a snowsuit, boots, socks, and a sweater, donated by the Canadian government.

The ICRC keeps supplies for use in emergencies at warehouses around the world. Here, supplies are being moved into a hospital in Iraq.

Despite all the planning and the individual delegates' experience, their work can quickly become unpredictable. Pierre Kraehenbuehl, now director of operations for the ICRC, led a group working in Peru in the early 1990s. They were holding a clinic in a marketplace when they were caught in the crossfire between guerrillas of the Shining Path rebel movement and a militia unit. Their work instantly turned from providing the poor with long-awaited medical attention to caring for the wounded.

Visiting Prisons

The Third Geneva Convention gives the ICRC the right to check that prisoners being held by either side in a conflict are being treated humanely. In 2002, the ICRC visited

448,063 detainees held in 2,007 places of detention in more than seventy-five countries.

In 2002, the ICRC inspected prison conditions at Guantanamo Bay Naval Station, where prisoners captured in the fighting in Afghanistan were being held by the United States. "They will look at the premises very, very carefully," an ICRC spokesman told the press in advance. "They'll check the water supply. They'll check the food. They'll check the living conditions, whether they have access to proper medical treatment, if required, and whether they can communicate with their families."

Prisoners taken by U.S. troops in Afghanistan in 2002 were held at Camp X-Ray at the Guantanamo Bay Naval Station on the island of Cuba. Prison conditions were inspected by the ICRC.

Many Americans, knowing the inspectors were coming, waited to read about what they found, but the ICRC does not issue public reports of its findings. "We can't give anyone anywhere an excuse to deny us access into a prison," the spokesman said.

By early 2003, the ICRC had handled more than 3,300 messages between internees at Guantanamo and their families. They also provided recreational materials, including books in Pashto, Russian, Chinese, and Tadjik, languages spoken by the prisoners.

In 1996, teenaged boys were combatants of the revolutionary United Front in Sierra Leone.

Child Soldiers

Three of every five individuals receiving aid from the ICRC are children. More than twenty-five articles in the Geneva Conventions and Protocols acknowledge the special task of protecting children during war. The Committee's work is not just helping children who are victims of war. It also deals increasingly with the terrible problem of child soldiers.

The 1977 Additional Protocols require that no one under the age of fifteen be taken into the armed forces of a country and participate in war. Some young boys, however, have found the idea of fighting in a war exciting. Also, in some parts of the world, such as southern Africa and Southeast Asia, many children are orphaned and homeless. Such boys—some as young as ten—are easily recruited into the military.

Jakob Kellenberger, president of the ICRC, observed in 2000, "Some of these children . . . are said to be capable of extraordinary heroism and of the most appalling crimes. Often they are not mature enough, in the depraved environment in which they live, to distinguish between good and evil. With no understanding of danger or death, it is they who carry out the most hazardous missions."

Families Torn Apart: The Missing

In the 1860s, Clara Barton began her search of Civil War battlefields to locate missing people. During the Franco-Prussian War in 1870, the

ICRC started the Central Tracing Agency when the delegates realized that a major part of the stress experienced by wounded or imprisoned soldiers was that their families had no idea where they were. Ever since then, an important part of ICRC activity has been directed toward connecting missing people with their families.

The delegates try to learn all they can about the missing people—where and when the individuals were last seen, what they look like, where they might go. As the delegates move throughout both sides of a conflict, they ask for help. During a two-year period in the Congo, the ICRC reunited more than six hundred children with their parents.

The many civil wars that are taking place throughout the world have torn families apart. The 1996 agreement ending the fighting in Bosnia-Herzegovina established an organization and process for locating missing people. By 2003, however, more than sixteen thousand people were still unaccounted for.

Almost two thousand Kuwaitis and Iraqis have been missing since the Gulf War in 1991. In 2003, the ICRC began a new major action called The Missing to raise awareness, help resolve the problems of missing people and their families, and prevent further disappearances.

In Sarajevo, Bosnia-Herzegovina, families continue to search Red Cross photo exhibits hoping to find missing family members.

Chapter Five

The Power of Humanity

Within the first forty days of 2003, the International Federation of Red Cross and Red Crescent Societies dealt with hardships caused by earthquakes in Afghanistan and Mexico; floods in Tunisia, Peru, Brazil, Madagascar, and Morocco; a cyclone in the Democratic Republic of Congo that left 1,700 homeless; bushfires in Australia; massive snow and an ice cap in Mongolia; the building of permanent food supplies in Ethiopia; a cold wave in usually mild Bangladesh; and immediate food aid in starving southern Africa.

RED CROSS RED CRESCENT

the *power* of **humanity**

In any one of these situations, the local Red Cross society and other national groups who come to help have to feed thousands of people, find temporary shelter for them, provide first aid to the injured, set up telephone information centers run by volunteers, and find ways to evaluate and distribute donations of food, clothing, and furniture.

Soldiers began a rebellion in the African nation of Côte d'Ivoire (Ivory Coast) in late 2002. The Côte d'Ivoire Red Cross Society, helped by the ICRC, immediately began to assist people who needed to be evacuated from war-torn areas. The aid workers had to

A tent city was assembled for people left homeless by an earthquake in Turkey in 1999. Providing housing for the displaced is a frequent activity of the Federation.

feed and try to shelter thousands of people left homeless. Thousands more refugees—perhaps a million all together—crossed out of Côte d'Ivoire into neighboring Mali, Niger, and Burkina Faso. These nations were not prepared for such a huge number of people. The International Federation took over.

In such a crisis, refugees generally stop immediately after crossing a border into another country. The Malian Red Cross provided victims of the Ivorian crisis with food and nonfood items, such as rice, cooking oil, sugar, soap, mosquito nets, and sleeping mats. When more refugees arrived, the Red Cross had to establish a larger, more permanent refugee center a long way from the border. The Spanish and the French Red Cross societies arrived to help.

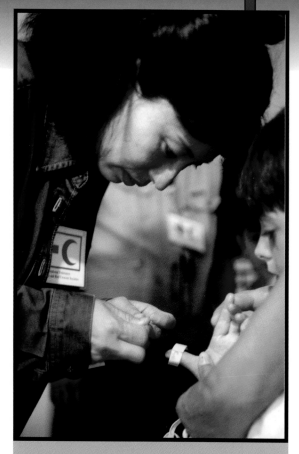

Societies help each other. The Japanese Red Cross Society sent volunteers to help the Albanian Red Cross feed, house, and care for the many ethnic Albanians fleeing the civil war in Kosovo in 1999.

The Need for Funds

In addition to supporting the local organizations with the immediate relief needs of the people affected, the Federation tries to establish changes that might prevent a similar disaster from being so serious later. The Afghan earthquake, for example, revealed the need for a new health clinic in an area where there had not been one. Until one was built, the medical volunteers at Red Crescent's mobile clinic did the work. They also rehabilitated five schools that were seriously damaged.

Depending on the Red Cross

Fifteen-year-old Shafi became head of his family when both of his parents died of AIDS. He and his three brothers are only four of almost a million orphans in Malawi. They are among those who receive a food ration, or allotted portion of food, every month. In the photo, Shafi has just fetched a 110-pound (50-kilogram) bag of maize, or corn, from a Red Cross distribution point. At home, he cooks *nzima*, the maize porridge that serves as the basic food for all Malawians. The only way Shafi has to earn money is by weaving mats. What he earns must be spent on food, so the boys have had no new clothes in the years since their parents died.

In any major disaster, emergency appeals to the public for donations of money, blood, and clothing are usually made. In most developed countries, these appeals are usually met with generosity. In addition, Red Cross and Red Crescent societies in every country hold an annual appeal, which builds up funds for the organization to run its regular programs and to prepare for the next emergency.

In addition, individuals, organizations, and nations can make donations to the IFRC itself. The donor can choose to give to a specific project, such as disaster preparedness or the Ethiopian food crisis, or to a general fund. Recently, the largest donor to the IFRC has been the United Kingdom, followed by Norway and Sweden. The United States is sixth. Most of the IFRC's annual budget of about $600 million comes from large grants given by the treaty countries.

The IFRC provides much more than immediate aid in a disaster. When the Assam River of India flooded in 2002, the IFRC provided aid to more than 14,000 families in three major ways: emergency relief, health care, and what is called capacity building. Capacity building, for example, includes helping the people of the Assam valley and the local Red Cross agencies increase their capacity or ability to handle the effects of another flood, even to the extent of building a flood-control dam. Capacity building also includes the buildup of permanent medical facilities.

Using their Skills

National societies often develop expert skills in one kind of struggle or another. The people in these societies prepare to use their skills around the world. Several societies, including the American Red Cross, have special skills in rehabilitating people with paralyzing injuries or illnesses.

The Bangladesh Red Crescent has great experience in dealing with cyclones. The society provides cyclone shelters to communities that are vulnerable to these storms. The shelters not only prevent death and injury from storms, but they also are used between storms as community centers.

The skills and experience of the American Red Cross are offered around the world with the international disaster response teams. In the three years after 1999, when the Response Team was started, it answered requests for assistance at disasters in thirty different countries.

The Red Cross has taken on the huge task of home-based care for the many people dying of AIDS in Zimbabwe, where it was estimated in 2003 that 34 percent of the adult population had become victims of HIV/AIDS.

In January 2003, for example, an earthquake in Mexico brought ARC volunteers from where they were stationed in Panama to help the Mexican Red Cross.

In additional to Red Cross or Red Crescent organizations, a major disaster or civil war draws out different nongovernmental organizations (NGOs) that want to help. Some are newcomers who are eager to help but may cause more problems than they solve because of inexperience. In 1994, the IFRC developed ten Principle Commitments the organization hopes all relief groups will follow.

Tornado Safety Tips

- Develop a Family Disaster Plan and supplies kit
- Identify safe places to go in case of a tornado (e.g. basement, room without windows)
- During a Tornado WATCH listen to a NOAA Weather Radio or local radio or television stations for updated information
- If you live in a mobile home, choose a safe place in a nearby sturdy building
- During a Tornado WARNING, go to a safe place immediately
- Stay away from windows
- If in a vehicle, leave it and go inside a sturdy, well-built building. If a building is not available, lie flat in a ditch or depression in the ground.

www.redcross.org

An American Red Cross health and safety promotion explains what to do in case of a tornado.

Peacetime Activities

It is important for any national Red Cross or Red Crescent Society to be prepared to deal with sudden disaster. Most of its time is spent on less dramatic activities. At any time, Red Cross or Red Crescent societies provide coffee to firefighters fighting house fires, provide blankets—or eyeglasses or shelter—to victims of fires, collect clothing and money for flood victims, organize **blood drives** to replenish local hospitals' supplies, and graduate new classes of qualified lifeguards and first aid workers. Perhaps the best known of these peacetime activities is the blood donor program.

One-third of all the blood donated in the world is given through Red Cross blood drives. The other two-thirds are provided along the guidelines used by the IFRC. In 1981, the IFRC, supported by the World Health Organization, developed a Code of Ethics for use in collecting blood.

Dr. Drew and the Blood Banks

Charles Richard Drew (1904–1950) was the American physician who developed the idea of blood banks. Before his work, donated blood had to be injected into an injured person soon after it was drawn because it could not be preserved very long, even under refrigeration. Also, the blood type of the donor and the receiver had to match. The world's first **blood bank** opened in 1936.

Drew developed a means of separating out the blood plasma (the yellowish fluid that carries blood cells) in large quantities. Plasma can be stored for longer periods than blood, and it can be used for anyone. In 1941, Drew became the first director of the American Red Cross's Blood Bank, preparing dried plasma for distribution to the armed forces. He resigned when the War Department decided that blood donated by white people had to be kept separate from blood given by African Americans. Drew's work formed the heart of Red Cross blood-donor programs the world over.

Other tasks carried out by community Red Cross volunteers vary by country. In the United States and Canada, the organizations support local food pantries, organize homeless shelters, help parents of young children anchor child-safety seats safely in their cars, provide first aid at large public gatherings, and even help travelers stranded in airports.

For Red Cross volunteers, the term "volunteer" doesn't necessarily mean that they don't get paid, as it might in some situations. It means that they are there of their own free will, not as required by some organization such as a military. Volunteers do not have to be adults. According to the American Red Cross, more than 40 percent of its volunteers are under age twenty-five.

Mental Health

One of the very important jobs the Red Cross has taken on in recent years is providing mental health workers to help victims of a disaster through the worst of the stress. On September 11, 2001, hijackers turned commercial aircraft into suicide bombs. They destroyed the World Trade Center in New York and part of the Pentagon in Washington, D.C. The

Thousands of Red Cross volunteers reported to New York City to help at the site of the World Trade Center bombings in 2001. This volunteer pauses in his task of helping the rescue workers deal with the fact that they are not finding anyone to rescue.

passengers made one plane crash in Pennsylvania to keep the plane from being used to destroy many more people.

Thousands of people died, but many more thousands survived, only to find themselves in severe emotional distress. The American Red Cross organized hundreds of trained mental health workers to help survivors begin to deal with the terrible loss and firefighters and rescue workers recover from the horrors of the things they had seen. In all, this terrible episode brought out the largest gathering of volunteers ever for a disaster relief operation: 54,577 workers arrived in New York.

In addition, because flights were cancelled into the city, supplies ran low. The American Red Cross joined with Amtrak and Coca-Cola to create the Clara Barton Express train. It carried in twenty thousand clean-up kits, twenty thousand hygiene kits, and beverages, plus two items not normally sent to disasters—eyedrops and dust masks—because of the dust in the air.

Working with Youth

Groups of young people, such as Boy Scouts and Girl Scouts, often learn first aid from Red Cross volunteers. Many people in many different settings learn CPR (cardiopulmonary resuscitation) skills from volunteers. Courses for babysitters and caregivers for the elderly are often arranged by community volunteers. Children are taught to swim safely, and as they grow, they are taught lifesaving techniques. Lifeguards at pools and lakes around the nation have passed American Red Cross tests.

In 2003, the American Red Cross signed an agreement with the Boy Scouts of America to make the Scouts an official provider of Red Cross health and safety programs. Three million Scouts will become additional trained first aid workers.

The Junior Red Cross has existed since 1917, when the war brought out about eleven million members in the United States. By the end of World War II, there were nineteen million members. During the 1950s, it became clear that the American Junior Red Cross program needed a change. In 1964, the name was changed to Red Cross Youth, and young people became volunteers.

Almost every Red Cross society in the world has a junior or youth program. Youth networks have been formed to encourage cooperation between young people in different regions of the world. The young people often go on to become the leaders of Red Cross and Red Crescent societies.

In 1953, this young man learned in a Red Cross aquatics class to turn his trousers into water wings to keep from drowning. He later became known as actor Clint Eastwood.

39

Chapter Six

Into the Third Century

In the autumn of 1942, the members of the International Committee met to discuss something they had learned. Germans were exterminating the Jews of Europe. The ICRC looked after the welfare of hundreds of thousands of prisoners of war, but Germany had regularly denied access to its prison camps. The Committee had evidence that Nazis were systematically rounding up and sending Jews and members of other groups from conquered countries to die in extermination camps.

Switzerland itself had recently made it very difficult for Jewish refugees from neighboring countries to cross into that mountainous country to reach safety. If the Red Cross took action and told the world what was going on, the Swiss organization would be going against the principles of both its nation and its own eighty-year-old rule of not taking sides in conflict. The Red Cross might also endanger its ability to reach and help prisoners of war.

The Committee asked whether it should do something, even though the members weren't sure what. Should they remain silent? One by one, the members spoke. They chose to remain silent.

Decades later, this decision is still being debated. Historians generally agree that even if the International Committee of the Red Cross had publicly condemned the exterminations, it would not have stopped Hitler from killing millions of Jews.

As World War II was ending, Allied soldiers found a few remaining Jewish prisoners in Nazi prison camps, where many Jews had been starved, tortured, and killed.

Caroline Moorehead, in writing about the ICRC's history, said, "The Committee's failure to speak out, to take the high moral ground in a way that is seldom offered to any one individual or any one organization, has haunted it ever since."

"Ethnic Cleansing" and IHL

Today, the doubt and uncertainty have not gone away, and there is little likelihood that it will in the future. During the war-torn 1990s following the breakup of Yugoslavia, bloody wars took place in Kosovo, Bosnia, and Serbia. Millions of Muslims were massacred by Serbian Christians. The *Christian Science Monitor* newspaper said, "The Serbs' frenzy of ethnic cleansing seemed to spit in the face of treaties that seek to set humane limits to modern warfare."

That writer and other international observers began to ask whether the Geneva Conventions were still relevant. Does it matter, in today's world, where traditional warfare ends and **genocide** begins?

The ICRC is convinced that International Humanitarian Law must continually be promoted. It hopes that continual emphasis on humanitarian law might persuade the world's people to bring about an end to war itself.

The Committee became concerned in 1999 that perhaps too many people think of the Geneva Conventions and humanitarian law as something Christian and Western. The ICRC set out on a search for local versions, with roots in local practice, to show that the Geneva Conventions are a universal expression of rules that everybody knows. The Committee uses local ideas to advance the thinking of the people.

In Guatemala, for example, Committee delegates talk of humanitarian law in terms of indigenous Mayan law and customs. In Somalia, they equate it to Somali warrior traditions. In Russia, the delegates call attention to the fact that a Russian general in 1776 ordered his men to treat prisoners in a humane way.

Breaking Away on Principle

Some people have thought that the ICRC's strict neutrality and determination not to speak out about what it finds have gone too far, that it has lost its humanitarian principles in the process. In the 1960s, a section of Nigeria called Biafra tried to separate from Nigeria. Some French doctors, delegates of the ICRC, were horrified at what they considered genocide, with the Nigerian government deliberately eliminating all the Biafrans it could. When the ICRC refused to let the French delegates speak out, the doctors broke away and formed a new organization, Doctors Without Borders (*Médecins Sans Frontières*). Its slogan is "Heal and Bear Witness." Doctors Without Borders was awarded the Nobel Peace Prize in 1999.

Facing Sharia

One problem facing the ICRC today involves the sharia law of some Muslim countries. Sharia is the system of law and practices of traditional Islam. Sometimes it calls for punishments that do not fit humane standards of today, such as amputating the hand of a thief or using torture as a form of punishment.

The Geneva Conventions, a 1982 resolution of the United Nations, and declarations of the World Medical Association have all said that doctors must not participate in corporal (bodily) punishment such as torture. The ICRC has decided to inform the people who are applying to work for the Committee that such situations may arise. If the applicants' personal ethics let them participate in corporal punishment, they are not hired.

The Emblem: Cross, Crescent, and ?

In 1876, Turkish soldiers killed a Red Cross worker in a Balkan war. The Committee's *Bulletin* said, "If the Cross is an emblem which speaks to the heart of Christians and commands their respect, it arouses, by contrast, wild passions in the Mohammedans [Muslims], and their instinct brings them to aim blows against it." The Committee accepted the use of the red crescent emblem in Muslim countries, though it was not mentioned in the Geneva Conventions until 1929.

Other nations have tried other emblems. For a while, Japan used a symbol consisting of two parallel horizontal rectangles. The Sudan proposed using a rhinoceros. Lebanon proposed a red cedar tree. From 1929 until 1980, Iran used a red lion backed by a red sun. After that, Iran changed its emblem to the red crescent. By 2000, twenty-seven nations around the world were using the red crescent instead of the red cross. However, some countries will not use either emblem, and these have remained outside the international structure because the Geneva Conventions require the use of one emblem or the other.

The Israeli national society, Magen David Adom (MDA), which might belong to the International Movement, has instead remained a nonmember because it refuses to use either the red cross or the red crescent as its symbol. The organization does similar work in health fields, but it

Magen David Adom sent assistance to the Congo after a volcanic eruption in 2002.

uses the Jewish Star of David (Magen David) symbol and thus has remained an "observer" at the international conference. Even though the MDA is very busy in its war-torn home, the organization has recently sent volunteers to work in earthquake-ravaged India and has carried donated supplies to the Congo when a volcano left thousands homeless.

The American Red Cross withholds part of its dues to the International Federation because of the Federation's refusal to consider including the Israeli medical aid society without a change in emblem. At the 2000 international conference, delegates took up the problem of the emblems. A working group was established, and it quickly decided that it would not accept Israel's Star of David as an additional emblem. Instead, conference members would create a new emblem to be used in special situations. By 2003, it looked as if the new, additional emblem would be a red diamond shape, white in the middle. It has no religious meaning that could offend anyone.

The new emblem has to pass the hurdle of being approved by two-thirds of the members of the international conference. It then needs to be written into an additional Protocol. It will be several years before the process is complete. In the meantime, most people around the world have come to depend on the emblems of the red cross or red crescent to see that humanitarian aid is on the way. The organizations represented by these emblems play a vital role in binding up the wounds of humankind.

A Sign of Hope

A Red Cross hospital in Hiroshima, Japan, was only partially destroyed by the first atomic bomb dropped in August 1945. Enough remained to treat some of the few humans left alive. In 1959, a monument was erected in front of the rebuilt hospital to the memory of the Japanese Red Cross members who died there. The inscription ends, "Henceforth all men know they must unite to abolish war and create the fraternal world where justice and peace shall reign. To this work the Red Cross will devote its enthusiasm and its faith."

1859 Henry Dunant observes the Battle of Solferino in Italy.

1863 International Committee for the Relief of Military Wounded is formed.

1864 Geneva Convention for the Amelioration of the Condition of the Wounded in Armies in the Field is drafted and approved.

1867 First International Conference of the Red Cross is attended by nine governments and the committees of sixteen nations.

1876 The symbol of the red cross on a white background is first used; the International Committee for the Relief of Military Wounded is renamed the International Committee of the Red Cross, or ICRC.

1899 Geneva Convention of 1864 is revised to include maritime warfare.

1906 Revised Geneva Convention created, called the 1st Convention

1907 Revised Geneva Convention changed to include maritime warfare, called the 2nd Convention.

1919 League of Red Cross Societies formed.

1925 First Geneva Protocol prohibits the use of poisonous gases in war.

1928 Statutes of the International Red Cross approved.

1929 Geneva Convention again revised. Geneva Convention related to the treatment of prisoners of war is adopted.

1929 The red crescent symbol on a white background is officially recognized for use in some countries.

1949 Four Geneva Conventions again revised.

1965 Seven Fundamental Principles of the Red Cross proclaimed.

1977 Protocols added to the Geneva Conventions to protect victims of international armed conflicts and noninternational armed conflicts.

1983 League of Red Cross Societies renamed League of Red Cross and Red Crescent Societies.

1991 League renamed Federation of the Red Cross and Red Crescent Societies.

1997 Seville Agreement between the ICRC and the IFRC signed.

2000 Draft protocol to create an additional emblem sent to governments.

Glossary

alleviate relieve

amelioration improvement, relief

amend repair or add to

autonomy the right of self-government

blood bank a refrigerated collection of various types of blood for use by hospitals and in emergencies

blood drive an organized campaign to persuade people to donate blood at a specific time and place

breach violation or break in terms of an agreement

chartered granted privileges by a government

genocide the mass murder or attempted mass murder of all members of a particular racial, ethnic, religious, or cultural group; also called ethnic cleansing

guerrilla warfare attacks by irregular or nongovernmental forces, often by individuals or small groups

hostage a person held captive to persuade other people to take some action

humanitarian having to do with the welfare of people

ideological having to do with ideas or theories about human culture

impartiality neutrality

lobby to try to influence public officials and the legislature

Nazis National Socialists, members of the German government between 1933 and 1945, led by Adolf Hitler

negotiate to talk back and forth until agreement is reached

nongovernmental organization NGO, an organization that works without government authorization

ratified approved

refugee a person who abandons home to seek safety, either in another country or in a safer part of his or her own country

To Find Out More

BOOKS

Bennett, Paul. *War.* The World Reacts Series. Smart Apple Media, 1999.

Noyed, Robert B., and Cynthia Fitterer Klingel. *Clara Barton: Founder of the American Red Cross.* Spirit of America Our People Series. Child's World, 2002.

Perkins, Ralf, and Kathleen Prior. *International Red Cross.* World Organizations Series. Watts, 2001.

Ransom, Candice F. *Clara Barton.* History Maker Biographies Series. Lerner, 2003.

ADDRESSES AND WEB SITES

International Committee of the Red Cross
19 avenue de la Paix
CH 1202 Genève, Switzerland   www.icrc.org/eng

ICRC Regional Delegation (covering USA and Canada)
2100 Pennsylvania Ave. N.W., Suite 545
Washington, D.C. 20037

International Federation of Red Cross and Red Crescent Societies
17 Chemin des Crêts, Petit-Saconnex, P.O. Box 372
CH-1211 Genève 19, Switzerland   www.ifrc.org

International Red Cross and Red Crescent Movement
                                        www.redcross.int/en

American Red Cross National Headquarters
431 18th St., N.W.
Washington, D.C. 20006   www.redcross.org
History of the American Red Cross:
          www.redcrossaustin.org/historyhtml/chapter1a.html

Index

Additional Protocols 24-25, 30
Afghanistan 29
Albania 33
ambulances 11, 14, 18
American Red Cross (ARC) 13, 15, 38-38, 44
Appia, Louis 9, 10, 12, 13
Arthur, Chester 13
Austria-Hungary 8, 11
AIDS 34, 35

Bangladesh 35
Barton, Clara 12-13, 14-15, 30
Battle of Solferino 8
Biafra 42
blood-donor program 36-37
Boardman, Mabel 15
Bosnia 27, 31, 41
Boy Scouts of America 39
Burundi 28

Central Tracing Agency 31
Chechnya 28
child soldiers 30
Colombia 26
Congo 31, 32, 43
Council of Delegates 18

Davison, Henry P. 15-17
delegations 20, 21
director-general 20
disaster relief 14, 15, 18, 19, 21, 32, 33, 35-36
Disaster Response Teams 35-36
Doctors Without Borders 42
Drew, Dr. Charles Richard 37
Dufour, General Guillaume Henri 9, 10
Dunant, Henry (Jean Henri Dunant) 5, 9, 17

Eastwood, Clint 39
emblems 18, 19, 28, 42-44
Ethiopia 34
ethnic cleansing 41
exterminations 40

first aid 39
France 33, 42
Franco-Prussian War 12, 13, 30
Fujimori, Alberto 4

Fundamental Principles 6, 7, 22
fund-raising 15-16, 34

Garfield, James 13
Gaza 23
Geneva 9, 11, 19, 21, 22
Geneva Conventions 11, 12, 13, 17, 18, 19, 24-25, 28-29, 41, 42, 43
Germany 16, 40
Gnaedinger, Angelo 20
Guantanamo Bay 29
Guatemala 18, 41

Indonesia 39
Italy 8, 11
International Committee (ICRC)
    founding 12
    responsibilities 22
    structure 20-21
International Criminal Court 25
International Federation (IFRC)
    founding 17
    responsibilities 22
    structure 20-21
International Humanitarian Law (IHL) 25-26, 30, 41
International Movement 5, 6, 7, 18, 20
Iran 43
Iraq 22, 23, 28, 31
Israel 43

Japan 11, 15, 33, 43, 44
Jews 40, 43
Jordan 22
Junior Red Cross 17, 39

Kellenberger, Jakob 30
Kosovo 33, 41
Kuwait 31

League of the Red Cross and Red Crescent Societies 17
Lebanon 6, 43
Lincoln, Abraham 12

Magen David Adom (MDA) 43
Malawi 34
Mali 33
Maunoir, Théodore 9, 10

Memory of Solferino, A 9
mental health 37
missing people 30-31
Moorehead, Caroline 23, 41
Moynier, Gustave 9, 10
Muslims 5, 42

neutrality 7, 24, 27
New York 13, 37
Nigeria 42
Nobel Peace Prize 42
nurses 16, 17

Ottoman Empire 11

Pennsylvania 14, 38
Pentagon 37
Peru 4, 11, 28
prisoners' rights 29, 41
Prussia 11

Red Cross Youth 39
refugees 18, 22, 27, 33
regional field offices 21
rehabilitation 33, 35
Rome Treaty 25-26

San Francisco 15
Serbia 11, 41
Seville Agreement 22
sharia 42
Spain 22, 33
Spanish-American War 14
Standing Commission 18-19
Sudan 43
Switzerland 9, 12, 19, 40

torture 42
Turkey 11, 19, 32, 42

United Nations 27, 42
United States 12, 13
U.S. Congress 14
U.S. Sanitary Commission 12

Washington, D.C. 12, 38
Washington, George 13
Wilson, Woodrow 15
World Health Organization 36
World Trade Center 37, 38

Yugoslavia 41

Zimbabwe 35